GRACE AND FORGIVENESS

GRACE & FORGIVENESS

JOHN & CAROL ARNOTT

Grace & Forgiveness
Published by Catch The Fire Books
272 Attwell Drive, Toronto ON m9w 6m3 Canada

Distributed worldwide by Catch The Fire Distribution. Titles may be purchased in bulk.
For information, please contact distribution@catchthefire.com.

Catch The Fire® is a registered trademark of Catch The Fire World.

ISBN 978-1-894310-75-8
Copyright © 2009 John Arnott

The Team: Emily Wright, Marcott Bernarde, Carlos Rodriguez, Sheena Gibbons,
Benjamin Jackson, Jonathan Puddle, Steve Long
Cover and interior layout: Marcott Bernarde (Catch The Fire)

Printed in Canada
April 2015

CONTENTS

FOREWORD

I consider it a privilege to write the foreword to this book. Reading it took me back to Westminster Chapel many years ago when John Arnott first preached for me there. I seldom opened my pulpit to a guest preacher on a Sunday morning, but I warmly welcomed John Arnott that day. It was a magnificent morning. John preached a message on forgiveness that I will never forget. I cannot remember being more pleased by a message than I was on that occasion.

Some people were surprised that I endorsed the "Toronto Blessing" (as London's Sunday Telegraph called it) which broke out in his church in Toronto during January 1994. I am sure some of my own people at Westminster wondered about my wisdom at the time. My vindication, if that is the right word, came by John's own preaching in Westminster Chapel. Everyone was enthralled. His message was theologically and biblically sound. The funny thing is, he preached on the very theme for which I myself have become somewhat known. I had preached and emphasized a teaching of "total forgiveness" for many of my years there, then came John with the same message! It was so powerful and fresh. Anybody present would be compelled to say that the ministry of a man who could preach a sermon like that was worth listening to, if not also taking a stand for—which I did and I have never been sorry.

The "Toronto Blessing" is not merely about people being blessed by the Holy Spirit. It is also about forgiving one's enemies and then being immersed in the Father's love. In other words, the blessing of the Holy Spirit is often in proportion to one's forgiving of others for the hurt and injustice inflicted on their lives. That is what this book is about.

Since being back in America after "retiring" I have preached alongside John on different occasions. I remember hearing him and Carol speak on the subject of forgiveness at a church in Texas. He brought out things I hadn't even thought of, things not in my own book and things I wish I had said! I even wondered if we should combine our books. But the nearest thing to that is my opportunity to endorse this book. This is why I am so thrilled to be a part of it.

We all have a story to tell. There will be readers who have been abused, lied about, betrayed, walked over, taken advantage of, hurt by their closest friend, let down by an authority figure—the list is endless. John and Carol give illustrations and reasons for forgiving that will make you want to forgive in a way you never dreamed possible. The greater the suffering, the greater the anointing. If you have suffered more than most, then you have a promise of blessing that is greater than that which is promised to those who have not been hurt as you have. Carol gives stories of personal forgiveness with stunning candor. She reveals the results of forgiving—how it leads to blessing beyond anything you would have anticipated.

This book will help you to forgive. It will change your life—forever.

R. T. Kendall

JUSTICE IS GOOD,
BUT MERCY IS BETTER

—JOHN ARNOTT

UNDERSTANDING GOD'S GRACE

No one can really understand God's love unless they understand the free gift of His mercy and His grace. And, paradoxically, no one can really understand God's grace without understanding what true love is all about—the nature of God's love towards us.

In everyday life we know that someone who is a true lover is very different from someone who is a pretender or a playboy. We know that true love should not be motivated at all by self-interest. And such is God's love for us. It is a love that seeks the very best for us; it is sacrificial; it never stops giving.

Perhaps the closest we can come to understanding the essence and quality of God's love for us—though it is still a faint reflection of the reality—is the way in which we love our children. We bring these helpless, fragile little things home from the hospital and we love them. They have not done anything to deserve our love, indeed they are totally incapable of doing anything for us, yet we love them. From the moment we become a parent we know that from now on, life will pretty much revolve around our child and often they will inconvenience us in ways we can only dream of! Yet, we never stop loving them—*really* loving them. Parents and their children are a model to help us understand the way in which our Heavenly Father God *really* loves each one of us.

As we think about how unconditionally we love our children and begin to grasp how complete and unconditional the Father's love for us is, we can begin to scratch the surface of His grace and understand a little of the motivation behind God's unmerited offer of salvation and forgiveness for our sins.

Despite a lot of good teaching on the subject in the Church over the years, many Christians are still mystified by grace. They fail to live in the richness of it themselves and they fail to show grace to others. Many are still trapped by a performance-based theology that thinks God's love must be earned or deserved. They think that if they behave well and perform good works for God then He will love them more. This is so far from the truth! God cannot love us any more nor any less than He does now, and He longs for us to live in the place of grace where we understand that He gives His love to us freely. God's love and grace are gifts for us to receive. Do we ever deserve them? No! We are totally undeserving, but we are the undeserving who are the apple of His eye.

GRACE AND FORGIVENESS

The title of this book *Grace and Forgiveness* is purposefully chosen because the issue of God's grace is vitally intertwined with the issue of forgiveness. They are not simply two distinct aspects of our spiritual life that we have decided to place together in the same book. When we come into a real understanding of the extent of God's grace towards us and what that means, we begin to see how vital and necessary it is that we pass that grace and love on to others. Grace becomes an irresistible force in our lives.

When properly understood, the "unfairness" and "injustice"

of God's grace towards us is deeply shocking, even offensive to our human understanding, as we will see. But in the same way that God lavishly and extravagantly pours His grace out upon our lives, He is calling us to learn how to show grace to others by forgiving those who truly don't deserve it. The great discovery of forgiveness is that, through a selfless act, we open ourselves up to a greater outpouring of the blessing of God on our lives.

There are two important things that every Christian needs to realize at some point in their journey as a believer, preferably sooner rather than later! The first is that our God is very big and very powerful and there is nothing that He cannot do. The second is that He is very loving and compassionate towards us. The Bible says that "God is love". This is not a statement about what He does, but about *who He is*. He is the very embodiment of perfect, flawless love. His heart for us is to see us living our spiritual lives where we are operating with the dynamics of His Kingdom, just as Jesus did. It is a Kingdom of love, filled with faith, aware of the bigness of our God; aware of His willingness to interact with us and do things for us as we act in loving obedience to Him. In this place, unconditional forgiveness becomes an essential part of our lifestyle and this paves the way for an even greater outpouring of God's mercy and grace upon us. But we must be aware that any *unforgiveness* in our life will have the opposite effect—it will short-circuit the power of the Kingdom in our life and will prevent the blessing of God from flowing. Unforgiveness is perhaps the number one grace blocker in a person's spiritual life.

Jesus made a definite connection in His teaching between faith and forgiveness. The more we delve in Scripture the more we see that if we are to have a dynamic faith that really works we must practice the gift of forgiveness.

Look at these words of Jesus in Mark chapter 11:

"'Have faith in God,' Jesus answered. 'I tell you the truth, if anyone says to this mountain, "Go, throw yourself into the sea," and does not doubt in his heart but believes that what he says will happen, it will be done for him. Therefore I tell you, whatever you ask for in prayer, believe that you have received it, and it will be yours.'"

MARK 11:22–24

So far so good. Many sermons focus on these three verses when the preacher is discussing the issue of faith and encouraging us to engage our hearts to believe and expect our great big God to act powerfully for us. And it is true that if we truly tap into His resources then nothing will be impossible for us—a great promise! But this is not the whole picture. There is another verse which ends this passage and completes what Jesus is saying here about faith:

"And when you stand praying, if you hold anything against any- one, forgive him, so that your Father in heaven may forgive you your sins."

MARK 11:25

Jesus was demonstrating that there is an unbreakable link between effective, faith-filled prayer and forgiveness or the lack of it. He is teaching us that yes, there is available a limitless potential in prayer for the person who places his trust completely in God and takes Him at His Word, but *only* if that person is free from unforgiveness in their life. Jesus wants us to know that if we are withholding forgiveness from others, then the action of faith in our prayer life will be crippled.

This is a very important principle for us all to learn. In the same breath Jesus is saying, "You can have whatever you want when you pray if you believe...but, by the way, if you have anything against anyone you better forgive them, because that issue can completely short circuit your faith."

Unforgiveness can not only leave our prayers unanswered, it can bring us into a place of loss where we forfeit the blessing of God. Consider for a moment the position of the person whose sins have *not* been forgiven by God. How effective will that person's prayers be? Mark 11:25 is not some optional extra suggested by Jesus for those who want to be super-spiritual. It is the all-inclusive, compulsory component of authentic faith. If we withhold forgiveness from others then God is obligated to withhold it from us—and that has dire consequences.

As I have meditated on this truth over the years, and studied the teaching of John Sandford which has been ground-breaking in this area, I have been able to see clearly that there are two distinct "realms" in which believers can live out their faith. I like to visualize these as two "levels" where Christians live depending on the choices they make in their lives. One is the *justice level* and the other is the *grace level*. They are intrinsically linked and in parallel, but in complete contrast to each other, like two sides of the same coin. On the one hand we have Law and justice, and on the other, mercy and grace.

LAW AND LOVE

The Law is good but mercy and love are better. Justice is good but grace is better. Let's examine the issue of justice and what it means for a person to live on the *justice level* as opposed to the *grace level*. Justice is a good, necessary thing that exists in the world, but mercy is better and is something altogether higher and richer in substance. We need to understand justice and why it has to exist before we can really appreciate mercy. The majority of the Western nations are founded on a legal system that has justice at its heart. The aim of the law is to attempt to administer justice appropriately and fairly and without prejudice.

One of the central principles of the justice system is that a person who commits a particular crime should receive a punishment befitting the seriousness of that crime. In that respect, all of us are very grateful for justice. If, for instance, someone breaks into our home and steals all our stuff, we are thankful that we can call the police and that we have some recourse if the culprit is then caught. Similarly, we are grateful that the police will come and protect us if our life is being threatened. There has to be a system of justice in society because it is foundational in holding society together. If justice breaks down then anarchy will reign.

The Bible teaches us that justice is an essential part of the character of God. Just as much as He is a God of love, He is just. Righteousness, justice and truth are central facets of His being. I recall that when the movie *The Passion of the Christ* was released, Time Magazine ran the following headline on its front cover: "Why Did Jesus Die?" To many people it is still a mystery. They think, "Some guy was crucified 2,000 years ago. Right or wrong, whoever He was, what difference does it make to me?" They don't understand that the cross was God executing justice for the sin of mankind. Behind the agony that Jesus endured on the cross was the impeccable, uncompromising, exacting, perfect *justice* of a loving God. It was so important that something be done about sin and injustice that God did the unfathomable. He came Himself as a man and willingly died on the cross. Your sin and mine was paid in full that day, but not by us, rather by the Son of God who loved us and gave Himself for us (Galatians 2:20). It was God saying, "What you have done to one another and all the injustice that exists in the world—it matters. So I have done something about it, something that you could not do for yourselves."

We know that God is very, very big, and yet He is also concerned with detail. Nothing, however seemingly insignificant, escapes His attention.

I like to think about how big God is. Consider the universe, this solar system we are in. It can take months, even years, for a space probe to fly from earth to one of the other planets orbiting around our sun—yet this group of planets, of which we are a part, is but a tiny speck in the galaxy we call The Milky Way, which is estimated to contain something like 200 billion stars and possibly as many as 400 billion.[1,2] Our sun is one of the lesser stars in this cluster. So here we are, but a speck of dust revolving around a lesser star and our galaxy is just one of hundreds of billions of galaxies in what scientists term the "observable universe". God holds all of this in His hand! Not only that, but the Bible tells us He knows every star by name. How can anyone know the name of 200 billion stars multiplied by many billion galaxies? God is very big and very smart, isn't He?!

Now go from the macro to the micro and zoom into your individual life as part of this vast, unfathomably large universe and realize that God has even counted and made a note of the number of hairs on your head! Can you grasp how precise and exact and awesome He is? Go under a microscope and see His perfection in terms of microscopic detail.

Now think again about the events of the cross through this filter of God's vastness and His precision. Scripture tells us that God so loved our world that He gave His only Son, that whosoever would simply believe in Him would not perish but have eternal life. Wouldn't it have been so much easier for God

1   Sanders, Robert. "Milky Way Galaxy Is Warped and Vibrating like a Drum." *UCBerkley News*. UCBerkley News, 9 Jan. 2006. Web. Retrieved on 24 May 2006. http://www.berkeley. edu/news/media/releases/2006/01/09_warp.shtml
2   Frommert, Hartmut, and Christine Kronberg. "The Milky Way Galaxy." *The Milky Way Galaxy*. SEDS, 25 Aug. 2005. Web. http://messier.seds.org/more/mw.html

to say, "Look, earth is a tiny little planet compared to the Universe. Things have gone wrong so let's just snuff it out and start again over here with a new group of beings." But even though God is perfect and His justice demanded payment for all the sins the human race had committed, and would ever commit, He is so loving, kind and compassionate towards us that His love prevented Him from simply wiping us out. Instead of executing His righteous judgment God said, "No, we have to put in place a plan to redeem them."

Every one of the vast accumulation of sins that mankind had committed and was compounding with yet more sin—wars, violence, sexual offences, occult activity—it all had to be paid for. God could not just sweep all that under the carpet and forget about it, because He is uncompromising in His justice and His integrity—but His mercy led Him to provide a Savior.

JUSTICE LEADING TO MERCY

God *must* be unwavering in His justice because He can never compromise His integrity. The foundation of His justice is the very immovability of God Himself. It is more solid than the ground we walk on. But God has issues with you and me! We are helpless to do anything about our sin on our own—we have no power to change the past—so God chose to execute His plan and send His perfect Son, His innocent One, to earth to take on the cloak of humanity and die in place of the guilty, allowing the guilty to go free. Jesus died to satisfy the justice of God, but through His death He laid the foundation for us to reach a higher level of living—the place of grace, the free gift of God.

Imagine the following scenario: a kid robs your house while you are out and ransacks the place, stealing all your valuables. Later the police catch him and eventually his case goes to court.

After all the evidence is heard the verdict is conclusive—he is found guilty of all charges. The judge says, "Young man, you have been found guilty as charged. You have to pay a fine of $50,000 or go to prison for five years." The guy says, "Your Honor, I don't have the money." "Fine," the judge says, "it will be five years in prison then."

In this scenario justice is being done. Remember, it's your house he robbed, thoughtlessly, with a callous disregard for you and your property. He destroyed all your possessions and the jewelry that was taken was never recovered because he sold it to some anonymous guy in a bar within a matter of hours. The thief was caught, however, and now he's getting what he deserves. You should feel glad about it because justice is being carried out. If he got away with a slap on the wrist, what good would that do? Next week he'd just do it again.

Justice has to be administered and a punishment meted out that is fitting for the crime because it provides a deterrent to the person who committed the crime, to dissuade them from offending again, and to others who might consider doing it themselves. If, for instance, a serial rapist was not punished appropriately and severely then what would deter him from doing it again?

There are some countries in the world that lack a strong sense of justice. When Carol and I first traveled to minister in Colombia we had three security guards assigned to us at all times because the local pastors were fearful of us being kidnapped and our family held to ransom. They were rightly concerned because justice in that nation has deteriorated badly and people have gotten away with committing a lot of crime without being properly punished. To experience a culture like Colombia's makes one appreciate the places in the world where law and order is much more apparent.

Once I was speaking about justice and mercy in a High

School, explaining to the kids there that Jesus, who knew no sin, died on the cross as a sacrifice for our sins that we might be forgiven. A young Muslim who was listening piped up, "That's not fair! God is fair, He would never do that!" I replied, "You may not think it's fair, but that is what love will do. Love's not fair."

Returning to our scenario, imagine if, as the Judge is about to seal the sentence and send this thief to jail, someone stands up in the courtroom and calls out, "Your Honor, this young man is a friend of mine and I believe he is truly sorry for what he has done. If it pleases the court, I will pay the fine for him." The Judge could exercise his discretion and legal authority and choose to accept payment from this third party—even though the person had nothing whatsoever to do with the crime. If that happened then the young man could be released and walk free. The crime would have been paid for, even though it was not paid for by the guilty one, but by an advocate who loved the guilty one enough to see him set free. That is precisely what Jesus did for you and me!

By this amazing action of God's grace Jesus is changing the face of the earth one person at a time. More than 1 billion on the earth have put their trust in Him and have been born again by the power of the Holy Spirit. Slowly but surely the Gospel is leavening the earth like yeast working its way through a lump of dough. Multitudes have come into the realization that they have no way out of their sins, no way of erasing the past even if they turned over a new leaf and began to live differently. There is only one answer, there is only one name under Heaven given to men by which they may be saved: the name of Jesus.

THE GRACE LEVEL

This sums up the message of the New Covenant. I, who am guilty, admit my sin and need of a Savior. He comes into my life at my invitation and I am raised to a new level where I don't deserve to be. I move from justice, where I should rightfully receive the full penalty for my sins, to grace where I can walk freely because of what Jesus has done for me. In the place of grace the river of God flows through my life—a river of blessing, of healing, of the impossible becoming possible. It is the river of the Holy Spirit. We access it by exercising childlike faith, believing in God's Word and putting our faith in Jesus.

Jeremiah prophesied that God would write a new covenant, one that would exist not on stone tablets like the old one, but one that would be written on the hearts of men and women. Under this new covenant the Law would no longer be like a straightjacket to us, constraining us, all about rules, regulations and good behavior. The axis of this new covenant would be a changed heart that aligns itself with the values of the heart of God. God does not spend all His time trying to be good; He is not constantly wrestling with a carnal nature; and He wants to invite us to live like that.

Ephesians 2:8 says,

> "For by grace you have been saved through faith, that not of yourselves, it is the gift of God. It is not of works lest anyone should boast. We are His workmanship created in Christ Jesus for good work which God prepared beforehand that we should walk in it. For by grace you have been saved."

Our English word "grace" is derived from the Greek word *charis*. We get words like "charity" from it—a gift given to someone who is undeserving in the sense that they cannot do anything to earn the gift, they just have to choose to receive it. Grace is just *given* to us—it is what happens when we put our trust in Jesus. When we accept God's gift of grace we are rescued by the Great Rescuer, Jesus our Savior. We move from being nowhere to occupying an incredibly privileged position in Christ—and all we did was simply believe. God did not require us to climb a mountain or swim an ocean to earn it—His grace was given to us freely.

THE PROBLEM OF SIN AND
THE COMMAND TO FORGIVE

As soon as we begin to talk about the free gift of God's grace in this way, the issue of sin and how we handle it soon rears its ugly head. "Sin" seems to be a word that people avoid using these days. Instead people prefer to say, "I have a problem" or "I made a mistake." Sin takes many forms, but in every case the root of it is selfishness. Sin is me doing something out of lust, greed and arrogance, usually at someone else's expense. It wounds that person and it wounds the heart of God.

I suspect that, like me, you tend to minimize your own sins of hurting others, but magnify the sins committed against you. When we hurt others we tend to say, "Oh, come on! Get over it, it's not that big a deal!" But when someone commits a similar offence against us, all of a sudden it develops into a major issue! "Do you know what he/she did to me?!" we cry. We have double standards when it comes to sin—we want mercy from God and others for all we have done wrong, but we want justice from Him for everyone else!

The Bible teaches us something very different. In Matthew 18 Peter approaches Jesus and asks Him a revealing question:

> "Lord, how often shall my brother sin against me and I forgive him? Up to seven times?"
>
> MATTHEW 18:21

Where did Peter get this idea from—that it would be

appropriate to forgive someone who sins against us up to, say, seven times before we wash our hands of them and have nothing more to do with them? Peter has been following Jesus around for a while now. He has seen that He is kind to prostitutes—He even let one kiss His feet for a prolonged time. Peter has grown up in Judaism, so he feels he has a very clear understanding of the Law, of justice, and of the penalties for sin. He knows that God does not tolerate sin and that every sin has to be paid for. Yet, at the same time, He sees Jesus being kind, understanding, compassionate and forgiving, towards even the dregs of society.

So Peter with his human logic comes up with a kind of confused compromise in mind. It is as though he is trying to find some middle ground between the Law's zero tolerance approach and Jesus' evident kindness and grace. He thinks, "What would be *reasonable* here?" Most of us, when people sin against us can tolerate a few offences committed by the same person, but if we're honest we tend to operate on a "three strikes and you're out" basis and even then it depends on the seriousness of the offence. We will put up with a few offences, but if it becomes a pattern then we will be very reluctant to trust that person again. Our natural inclination is to protect ourselves from being hurt again and effectively cut them off. Peter at least goes beyond this attitude. Perhaps he thinks he is being super-tolerant by saying, "OK, how about if I was to forgive a person seven times? Would that be good, Jesus?"

I would have loved to witness this conversation as it took place. I would have liked to see the look of utter astonishment on Peter's face as Jesus replied, "Not seven, but seventy times seven!" Jesus must have smiled at Peter. Peter was so wide of the mark—he didn't understand the application of grace at all. To challenge his assumption Jesus threw back a much larger number than Peter had imagined. In effect He was saying, "Seventy multiplied by seven would be more like it, Peter, but actually you go on forgiving people indefinitely." Jesus knew that grace is the *only* place for believers to live and, no matter what, you don't want to find yourself living back on the justice level. To make His point crystal clear, however, He told His disciples the following parable.

THE UNMERCIFUL SERVANT

"Therefore, the kingdom of heaven is like a king who wanted to settle accounts with his servants. As he began the settlement, a man who owed him ten thousand talents was brought to him. Since he was not able to pay, the master ordered that he and his wife and his children and all that he had be sold to repay the debt."

MATTHEW 18:23–25

Let's put what this man owed into context. A talent is a unit of weight that was used in biblical times and was the largest measure of silver (or gold) in use before the introduction of coins.[3] All business dealings at that time required the movement of vast quantities of silver. One talent was between 60-80lbs of silver—that is a lot of silver. So imagine, this man owes 10,000 × 80lbs of silver. Let's convert that into today's money. If you were to go out and buy a bar of silver it would weigh 1,000 Troy ounces or 68.58lbs, roughly the equivalent of one talent. That bar of silver would cost you $10.82 per ounce i.e. $10,820 in total. So the man in Jesus' story owed the equivalent of $108,200,000 US!

It was an immense amount of money and the man had absolutely no way of paying it back. Anyone hearing Jesus' story knew that beyond doubt. The master ordered that the servant and his wife and children be sold into slavery so that

3   Bromiley, Geoffrey William. *International Standard Bible Encyclopedia.* Grand Rapids, MI: W.B. Eerdmans.

the debt would gradually be paid off. But, of course, it was such a huge debt that they would be slaves for the rest of their lives.

Have you ever had a bank loan and gotten behind with your payments? If so you will understand only too well that the bank knows nothing about mercy! As far as they are concerned the law is the law and justice is justice! That is what Jesus wants to illustrate here. But then, there is a twist in Jesus' story when the servant begs for mercy. Verse 26 says,

> "The servant fell on his knees before him. 'Be patient with me,' he begged, 'and I will pay back everything.'"

The servant was begging his master for mercy and for time to pay the debt back. The master was moved by compassion and then we read this incredible verse:

> "The servant's master took pity on him, canceled the debt and let him go."
>
> MATTHEW 18:27

Not only did the master grant the servant mercy, he forgave him the debt altogether—wiping the slate clean! Anyone who has ever had a serious bad debt in business will appreciate what an act of grace this is—especially regarding such a vast amount of money as Jesus is talking about. When I was in business myself, Dick, my accountant would come and see me every year to discuss my accounts and he would want to write off any bad debts that were hanging over from the previous year. One year he told me, "We have $20,000 of bad debts here. I want to write it off the books." My immediate response was, "Dick, you can't just write it off! This is $20,000 of our money!" But Dick said, "Well, this one has died, this one has moved and we can't trace him ... you're not going to get the money so you might as well write it off." I understood very clearly, at that point, that "writing off" a debt meant that *I had paid for it!* I took the hit and the money came right out of my pocket—the other person had gotten away without paying their debt.

Similarly, in Jesus' story the master is saying, "I will pick up the tab for this. You owe me millions but there is no way you can pay. I would have to sell you, your wife and your kids and it would still fall far short. I will pay the debt myself and you will be released." This is exactly what Jesus went on to do for us at the cross. We had no possible way of paying for our sin, so He did it for us.

The servant who found mercy must have gone home to his wife that day and had a fabulous celebration. Imagine having such a huge debt hanging over the family, day after day, week after week. They must have been constantly bogged down with thoughts of, "how are we ever going to be free of this?" Then one evening the husband walks through the door and tells his wife, "We're free! We are not in debt anymore!" They must have celebrated for a long time. However, things turned bad for the servant pretty quickly when he subsequently went out and sought out a fellow servant—a man who owed *him* some money. We read that,

"When that servant went out, he found one of his fellow servants who owed him a hundred denarii. He grabbed him and began to choke him. 'Pay back what you owe me!' he demanded. His fellow servant fell to his knees and begged him, 'Be patient with me, and I will pay you back.' But he refused. Instead, he went off and had the man thrown into prison until he could pay the debt. When the other servants saw what had happened, they were greatly distressed and went and told their master everything that had happened."

MATTHEW 18:28-30

This man's fellow servant owed him a paltry sum of money compared to the debt which he himself had been released from. One hundred denarii was the equivalent of four month's wages or about $10,000. Yet, the servant who had just been forgiven 10,000 times more than this decided to show no leniency to his fellow servant. Other servants of the master's household got to hear about this and in no time the servant was back in front of his master.

> "'You wicked servant,' he said, 'I canceled all that debt of yours because you begged me to. Shouldn't you have had mercy on your fellow servant just as I had on you?'
>
> In anger his master turned him over to the jailers to be tortured, until he should pay back all he owed."
>
> MATTHEW 18:32–34

We know, of course, that the servant should have followed the example of his master, shown mercy to his contemporary and forgiven his debt. What is truly shocking in this verse is how the debt that was "forgiven" by the master is suddenly reinstated and the full force of the master's wrath is brought to bear on the unmerciful servant. But then Jesus delivers the punch line of the whole story to us:

> "So my heavenly father also will do to you if each of you from his heart does not forgive his brother his trespasses."
>
> MATTHEW 18:35

CHOOSING JUSTICE OR MERCY

This has very serious implications for all of us, doesn't it! Can I have mercy for me and justice for you? No way! We can have justice or we can have mercy, one or the other, but we cannot pick and choose or have both.

Justice was encapsulated in the Old Testament Law by the phrase "an eye for an eye and a tooth for a tooth." If someone was to strike another person and blind them in one eye, the Law took the view that the offender should also have one of his eyes put out. In this way the offended party was "compensated" for his loss and the two were put back on "equal" terms. Hopefully the perpetrator learned the needed lesson. In modern times compensation is paid in financial terms instead, but the basic principle continues. If we want mercy, however, we have to move to a higher plane of operation, to live to a higher standard. Under grace what happens if someone comes along and puts out my eye? Or what happens if someone comes along and commits any kind of offence against me? In a word: nothing! We choose to forgive that person and to leave the issue of justice in God's hands. It is that simple.

"But life is *not* that simple!" someone will protest. I totally understand that sentiment, because what worries us most about forgiving someone who sins against us, is the thought that "they are just getting away with it". We can sometimes feel that God is standing by doing nothing whilst we are being wronged and because we are commanded to forgive then the other person is getting away scot free. This is why often people will "take the law into their own hands" and take action to "even things up". But this is not what the Bible teaches we should do. When we respond to hurt and offense by taking revenge—for that is what it is—the devil is pleased because he says, in effect, "I'm so glad you've decided to take revenge on that person, because you have just left the place of grace and come back down into justice. Now I can demand that you repay everything that *you* owe!" Your former (forgiven) debt is reinstated.

When we decide to stop living in grace and execute judgment on someone else, like the unmerciful servant, we are making a choice that has serious ramifications. Effectively we are choosing to step outside of the blessing and protection of God and deliver ourselves to "the torturers", in other words giving Satan license to reinstate the "debts" we owed and hold them against us. This may sound harsh to many, but it is what Jesus clearly teaches about the result of unforgiveness.

At all costs then, we want to remain living in grace. In grace a completely different dynamic is in operation that the devil knows nothing of. When someone sins against us, we forgive them and choose not to hold onto that offense or our own hurt. We release them completely, and move on, choosing to apply God's grace to the situation, or as one pastor put it, "Say grace to it." But what of the other person who sinned? Do they get away with it? Our human reasoning says, "Lord, did you see that? If I forgive that person they will get away with that kind of behavior all the time!"

God, however, responds by saying, "I saw the sin and I will deal with that person one day, but that is my responsibility, not yours, child." We have to trust God to administer justice as He sees fit in His time. We don't take the matter into our own hands. Instead, we must choose to remain in God's river of grace, remembering how big He is and how loving, kind and patient He is with us when we fall. Living by grace dictates that even though someone wounds us deeply, we choose to forgive them for what they have done. We have a heavenly Father who watches over us and even knows the number of hairs on our head. He will heal our hurts and restore us when we are wounded. He will probably even bless us abundantly more than we expect, just for being obedient, because that is His nature.

In grace we can never lose. It is hard to emphasize this

point enough! It is so important that we grasp this principle and live in the truth of it. Please note, I am not saying that justice should not be done in your life or that it is possible to simply forgive anyone who does anything to you without a thought. If, for instance, someone is abusing you, then you have to follow a course of action which prevents that from happening again. God is not asking you to continue being abused. But you can still, ultimately, forgive that person for what they have done and, indeed, you must do so in order to live in freedom and not be dragged back down to live on the justice level.

There are many Christians walking around today who wonder to themselves, "Why does everything seem to go wrong in my life? Why is the devil always after me? Why does there seem to be a curse over my life?" They are trying to work out why there doesn't seem to be any protection over their life. In many cases this will be because they have made poor choices in their relationships with others and chosen to "bury" the hurt and bitterness of past offenses instead of forgiving and releasing these to God. By their choices they have made themselves vulnerable to attack. By withholding mercy from others and exercising unforgiveness they have stemmed the flow of God's blessing and protection over their lives, leaving them open to assault from demonic forces. Even if someone does the most terrible thing to you, you must never go back to the justice level. It must be *grace, grace, grace.* Leave justice with God. Don't allow your heart to become hurt, bitter and unforgiving. Trust instead in His love, grace and blessing toward you.

For anyone who is still thinking, "I'm not sure..." look at the words of Jesus in Matthew 6:9 as He teaches His disciples how to pray: "*forgive us our debts as we forgive our debtors.*"

Jesus placed the giving and receiving of forgiveness at the absolute center of the Christian life. We simply cannot take forgiveness for ourselves but withhold it from others. Jesus underlines this point immediately after concluding the words of the model prayer:

> "For if you forgive men when they sin against you, your heavenly Father will also forgive you. But if you do not forgive men their sins, your Father will not forgive your sins."
>
> MATTHEW 6:14-15

His words are as clear as they can be. We either live in grace or we live in the realm of justice, demanding our rights and taking the consequences of our sin. Compared to that, grace and mercy is a fantastic deal! I don't know about you, but I certainly do not want to get what I deserve!

A WORD ABOUT NEGATIVE THOUGHTS AND WORDS

In the next section are some short accounts of the experiences others have had when they decided to forgive. But before that, let's look briefly at the role that our own negative thoughts and words play in the practice of forgiveness.

Having been a pastor for a long time I have found that little depletes the energy and resources of a person more than the woundedness which they carry around in their heart. People can become so inwardly focused on their own hurt that they have no time or energy to give of themselves to others. When someone is trapped in such a cycle they are effectively prevented from progressing in their spiritual life; they are so focused on simply getting through "today" that tomorrow never enters the equation.

The problem is, when we are inward looking, wrapped up in our own hurt, we don't allow ourselves to be open to the healing, restoring touch of God and the enemy can have a field day as he sows one negative thought after another into our minds and hearts. The more we harbor such negative thinking, the more that thinking will show up in our speech, resulting in the kind of critical, judgmental words we know we are seeking to avoid.

Some years ago my friend, Mark Virkler, wrote a course called *Pure in Heart*. One module of that course was called *Discerning the Accuser from the Comforter*. In it Mark made the incredible comment that "every negative thing and thought is always of the enemy, and every positive, life-giving, uplifting thought is always of the Holy Spirit." Mark asserted that the Holy Spirit was always positive while the enemy was always negative.

God can speak to us in any way He chooses, but He often chooses to do so in a "still, small voice" that comes to our consciousness like a thought. Often when we have a thought that is pure, righteous and positive it is simply the Holy Spirit talking to us. When I first heard Mark's teaching it came as a shock to me that the devil tries to work in the same way. He also whispers "thoughts" into our minds, but of course, these messages are in opposition to the life-affirming direction of the Holy Spirit. The accuser accuses and the Comforter comforts. Simple, but profound.

This whole teaching developed out of the conviction Mark had that in his own life, at least 80% of the time his thoughts were negative, critical and judgmental. Only 20% were positive. During the teaching of the module he tested all those present and discovered that the same was true for most people.

If you listen to the conversations that people have, Christian or otherwise, one notices that most of the talk is negative. People talk about the injustices that have been committed against them and rehearse their hurts and grievances. They hardly focus at all on the positive aspects of their lives. Little

JUSTICE IS GOOD, BUT MERCY IS BETTER

wonder then that so many are missing out on the fullness of the blessing of God.

SPEAKING LIFE

Because of our pride and independence we think that have enough wisdom to make fair and honest judgments in every situation of life. Something happens to us and we make our assessment of that situation, then we begin to speak it out. But the truth is, when we judge we are usually heavily biased. Our judgments tend to be based on limited information and we are usually negative and unfair. When we judge others it almost always comes out as an accusation. We judge and accuse others and unwittingly find ourselves in agreement with the "accuser of the brethren".

Instead we need to take our speech in the opposite direction. Instead of judging and accusing others we need to build others up, encourage and edify them. We must bless and not curse, forgive and not accuse. We have to take steps to take captive our negative thoughts. My prayer is continually, "Lord, I would like the numbers to be turned around. At the very least, help me to be only 20% negative and 80% positive." That would be more like it.

Settle this issue in your heart. The Holy Spirit is always positive and Satan is always negative. That sounded extreme to me the first time I heard it. I had to process that information for several weeks before I concluded that even when God brings discipline and correction to our lives He do so to take us in a positive direction and save us from ruin. His intent is always life-giving and redemptive. So remind yourself constantly to speak life to others.

STORIES OF THE POWER
OF GRACE AND FORGIVENESS

Once I was speaking in Winnipeg on the topic of forgiveness and at the end of the meeting I was approached by a man who was literally trembling with emotion. He said very aggressively, "You don't know what you are asking of me!" I replied, "Sir, I've been a pastor for a long time and I've heard a lot of stories—tell me your story." He told me about the terrible things that had happened in his family. He had discovered that his three year old daughter had been sexually abused by his own father. His little girl was completely traumatized and was having constant nightmares. The whole matter was in the hands of the family court and his entire family had been torn to shreds over night. He demanded to know, "Now you're telling me that I have to forgive my father?"

I felt heartbroken for this poor man. I said to him, "Sir, I'm not telling you that you *have to forgive him*. Forgiveness is not me taking the truth of the Gospel and holding it like a gun to your head. I am not saying, 'forgive or else.' When you are able to forgive your father your forgiveness needs to be a gift—that is what grace is. But I can promise you this—if you don't begin working through this issue, eventually it will eat you alive, and twenty years from now you will still be as angry as you are tonight and your twenty-three year old daughter will be messed up."

Sin is a horrible, ugly thing. It is occurring everywhere in the world right now, but when it touches our lives like this, then we truly understand its destructive power. I wish I could tell you that this young man chose to forgive and that the course of his and his family's life changed that day—but the truth is, I don't know what he decided to do. I just hope that he took the path of forgiveness so that his family could begin a process of being released from the inevitable downward spiral they were facing.

To demonstrate the power of what can happen when people do decide to forgive, I want to recount several real life instances that we have come across in ministry. These are people whose lives were changed for the better when they made a decision to forgive and live in grace instead of justice.

HEALING THROUGH FORGIVENESS

When R.T. Kendall was the pastor of Westminster Chapel in London he invited me over to preach on one occasion. It was an honor for me to step into that pulpit where so many great evangelical preachers had stood before. I spoke about the importance of forgiveness. At the end of the meeting, one of the ladies in the church came to me and told me her story.

She was a nurse. Seven years earlier, while she was making her way home from work one night, at around 11 PM a man attacked her. She was dragged into an alleyway where he raped her and then tried to beat her to death with a steel pipe. He left her for dead, but amazingly she survived the ordeal. Numerous bones had been broken in the assault and she had been left deaf through the numerous injuries to her head. She had lived in constant emotional and physical pain ever since.

It was through her deafness that she first began attending Westminster Chapel. Louise Kendall conducted a regular outreach ministry to the deaf members of the community. This lady had come into the church and found Jesus, and now she was a member of the church.

After the meeting this dear one came to see me in the vestry and told me, "I want to pray with you. I want to forgive the man who did this to me, because I see that it's my only way out." When such a violation of a person occurs an ungodly soul tie is formed that binds you to the memory of what happened, and to the anger, bitterness and hatred that you have towards this person who ruined your life. We can all understand how this happens and sympathize with the person, but wouldn't it be an awful tragedy if, years and years later, the person who violated them still had the power to continue destroying their life? This lady realized that, for her own sake if nothing else, forgiveness was the only way to be free of that power—not so this man could "get away" with what he did, but for her own good, so that she would be free at last.

We said a short prayer together and just as we were concluding, suddenly the lady's bones began to rearrange and we could both hear audible cracking noises. She cried out in alarm and I asked her, "What's happening?" All she could manage in reply was, "My body!" Following the attack her rib cage had healed all wrong and was one of the major causes of the constant pain and discomfort she suffered. Now it was cracking and shifting around into the correct position as God healed her. In a matter of minutes she was completely pain free. It was an amazing miracle. R.T. Kendall subsequently wrote to me a number of times about that lady because she was such a great testimony to the power of forgiveness. She had left the justice level and entered up into the grace of God. The minute the barrier of unforgiveness was removed, the healing river of God came flooding in. She left the meeting that morning one happy lady.

REDEMPTION
THROUGH FORGIVENESS

Then there is the story of Dick, whose son was shot dead by a drug dealer who had mistaken his son for someone who owed him money. The police caught the young man who pulled the trigger and he went to prison. Dick got justice, but that didn't bring his son back. Dick was being eaten up, constantly turning over the events in his mind whilst mourning the death of his son. He felt such anger towards the person who had taken his son's life away, but one day God spoke to him and said, "Dick, there is only one way you are going to be free. You are going to have to forgive."

Of course, Dick protested, "But they don't deserve to be forgiven, Lord!" But God replied, "I know, Dick, but neither did you." This turning point enabled Dick to travel on a new road, towards forgiveness. The road was long and hard and space doesn't permit me to tell all the details, but one day Dick finally got to the point where he knew he had to forgive the young man who had murdered his son and he was willing to do so. He decided to write a letter to the young man in prison and he enclosed a New Testament.

For his part, the young man in prison was full of remorse, and later recounted how he tortured himself daily with the question, "Why did I do it?" He knew that he had ruined his life. He had sought some kind of solution by going to the prison chapel, but he wasn't getting anywhere. He even prayed for forgiveness, but the heavens were brass. He just could not see how God could possibly forgive him for what he had done. But then he received Dick's letter, which read, "I am the father of the young man you murdered. I want you to know that I am a Christian and that I forgive you for what you did." Dick's words so broke this young man that he fell on his face and wept.

Against lawyers' advice, Dick and this young man began corresponding with one another. They wrote to each other for a long time, until one day Dick decided that he wanted to go to visit him in prison. In due course a meeting was arranged which would take place in the prison chapel. On the day they met, Dick's opening words to his son's killer were, "I'm the father of the young guy you shot and I'm here to wash your feet." At this, the young man broke down and wept. "I can't let you wash my feet!" he protested. But Dick insisted, explaining, "You need to understand ... I need to do this for my own healing. So, please, let me wash your feet." That day in the prison chapel both men washed each other's feet, weeping together as they did it.

Later Dick was able to tell me, "You know, John, that boy has become like a son to me. God has so changed him. He is no longer the same guy who pulled the trigger. He's been forgiven, redeemed and God has renewed him. So if Jesus has accepted him, how can I not accept him?"

AN UNEXPECTED HEALING

The apostle Paul made an important point about the connection between healing and wholeness and making ungodly judgments. In 1 Corinthians 11, speaking specifically about discerning the Lord's body during communion, he says, "*he who eats and drinks unworthily eats and drinks judgment ... for this reason many are sick among you and many sleep* [meaning, have died] *for if we would judge ourselves we would not be judged.*"

"If we would only judge ourselves instead of judging others," Paul says, "then we would not be suffering from sickness and even dying prematurely." What does judging ourselves mean? It means we realize that we are little different from the person who has sinned against us—we are both in dire need of God's mercy. We can suffer needlessly when we don't "get" the message of grace.

I remember praying for an older man named Fred who was injured in a car accident fifty years before I met him. I asked him whose fault the accident had been and he told me, "It was the other guy's fault." I asked Fred, "Did you ever think of forgiving the guy for smashing into you and injuring you, ruining your life?"

"No," he replied, "it never occurred to me."

We prayed a short prayer together and then Fred prayed, "Lord, I forgive the guy who caused this accident and left me in pain for fifty years. He owes me nothing. The grace of the Lord Jesus Christ is sufficient for me." At that moment Fred left the justice level and entered into the fullness of God's grace. As he did so, the power of God flowed into him and all the pain left his body. At that point, Fred's daughter, who was accompanying him, screamed and collapsed in utter shock. She told us later, "I have never seen my father do that!" Fred was stretching and bending over, testing out his newly healed body, something his daughter had never seen him do in living memory!

Very often unforgiveness is the reason why miracles don't happen. It is one of the great grace blockers. But Fred's story illustrates for us the kind of thing that can happen once grace is unleashed.

PUTTING GRACE INTO ACTION

We tend to have lots of reasons why we should not forgive people. We say, "They don't deserve to be forgiven." Well, that's true—they don't. We protest: "Why should they get away with it?" Now we have to trust God and realize that, in the end, no one gets away with anything. But how about you? Do you want to be bound by unforgiveness and block the blessing of God in your life? Will you allow it to rob you of the love, joy and peace that your Heavenly Father has for you?

The Gospel only works in grace. When we enter into grace we receive the added bonus that the devil cannot follow us there. That is the part about grace that I love the most. The enemy will always try to do things to pull us back down into the justice level, but if we choose to say, "Lord, I am living in grace, I'm not going there," then even if it costs us everything, we still win.

UNLOCKING JUDGMENTS
(The Hidden Key)

—CAROL ARNOTT

FORGIVENESS IS NOT AN OPTION

In Matthew's Gospel Jesus states very clearly that in our lives forgiving others is not an option, but a vital necessity. The reason He puts forward is a very good one and it has more to do with us than it does the people we are forgiving: *If we withhold forgiveness from those who have hurt us, no matter how well justified we feel in doing so, we are creating a barrier that will prevent the grace of God flowing into our life.*

Jesus told a parable about a servant who was forgiven a great debt himself and yet refused to forgive a minor debt owed to him by a fellow servant. This man, Jesus said, was "*turned over to the jailers to be tortured, until he should pay back all he owed.*" It was an impossible task, because the servant owed an unfathomable sum of money. Then Jesus applied the principle to you and I personally:

> "This is how my heavenly Father will treat each of you unless you forgive your brother from your heart "
>
> MATTHEW 18:35

Anyone can understand this simple, direct verse—it means what it says: as long as we refuse to forgive others we are effectively blocking the receiving of God's grace and forgiveness for ourselves. But many people seem to struggle with this part of Jesus' command: ... forgive your brother *from your heart*. Notice it does not say forgive them "in your head" or even "just say that you forgive them and it'll be OK." Our forgiveness must be genuine and heartfelt. We have to mean what we say, not just go through the motions!

We read similar commands in other parts of Scripture. The writer of Hebrews tells us to,

> "Make every effort to live in peace with all men and to be holy; without holiness no one will see the Lord. See to it that no one misses the grace of God and that no bitter root grows up to cause trouble and defile many."
>
> HEBREWS 12:14−15

MY RELATIONSHIP WITH MY MOTHER

When I first became a Christian the verses above presented themselves as a real challenge to me. As soon as I heard the words of Jesus speaking about forgiveness I came to the difficult realization that I needed to forgive my mother. To put it mildly our relationship was not good and I knew that I had that "bitter root" inside me which, if not dealt with, would strangle my faith and cut me off from the grace of God.

The problem was, I didn't need to forgive my mother for just one or two unfortunate incidents in the past where I had held on to the offence. Without exaggeration, there were at least a thousand different things I needed to work through because my relationship with her was so dysfunctional and difficult for the majority of our lives.

Growing up as a little girl I was unaware of the events and influences that had shaped my mother's life. All I knew was that from my perspective she was unpredictable and volatile. I could never guess when she might explode with anger, it would just happen, over and over again, and often for seemingly insignificant reasons. Once I had a group of girlfriends over and we spent the afternoon in my bedroom giggling about nothing, just having fun and laughing together. Later my mother questioned me saying, "Why were you laughing?" I said, "I don't know, Mom, we were just laughing about nothing." Her temper flared immediately and she yelled at me, "No you weren't, you were laughing at me!" Despite my protests, and me trying to tell her that I was not laughing at her, I got the strap—and the strap would always involve bruises and welts—it was not a spanking, but a serious beating.

My mother would regularly explode into anger for no apparent reason and she would control and dominate me through that anger. Consequently, as I grew up I learned to hate her. Outwardly I wasn't rebellious to her, I was too afraid of her violent tendencies to be rebellious, but in my heart I hated her with a passion. So I lived a facade of being nice to her whilst secretly I longed to escape.

But now, as an adult and a brand new Christian, I began to work through the catalog of offences that had accumulated over the years. I forgave my mother for this, and many other things, and I worked my way down the list. Yet, despite my best efforts, something was still not right. I didn't really feel like I had truly forgiven her. It was then that Jesus' words struck home, "... *unless you forgive from your heart*..." and I understood that whilst I had sought to carry out the process of forgiveness in my head, my heart had not been involved. I realized that I had no love for my mother in my heart, so how could I have truly forgiven her?

I talked to God about this saying, "Lord, maybe I didn't really mean it when I said it? Maybe I just forgave her out of duty—because I knew it was the right thing to do?" So then, because I wanted to be obedient to God and do what was right, I tried to work through each of those one thousand issues again, but this time really trying to mean what I was saying, putting everything I could into the words.

It was a good beginning, and helpful to be sure, but sadly, at the end of this process, in my heart I still didn't love my mother. Now I was exhausted and exasperated. "Lord," I prayed, "there still has to be something wrong, but I don't know what else to do. I know that I probably have a thousand things that I need you to forgive me for, and I don't want to block your grace in my life, but I just don't know how to make these words go from my head to my heart."

THE MISSING KEY

I was very frustrated. Since I was a young girl all the way into adulthood I had hated my mother, and I had to be honest with myself and admit that despite my best efforts, that fact had not changed. I still hated her in my heart. As a Christian, however, I did not want this and I did not want to miss out on God's blessing in my life. I knew that I had to do something. Then I read this verse in Deuteronomy and a light came on in the distance at the end of my black tunnel as the Holy Spirit gave me revelation:

> "Honor your father and your mother, as the Lord your God has
> commanded you, so that you may live long and that it may go well
> with you in the land the Lord your God is giving you."
>
> DEUTERONOMY 5:16

I discovered the key to my problem in this verse. In the areas of my life where I had been left hurt, wounded and angry by my mother's actions, I had pronounced judgment upon her and dishonored her name. As long as those judgments remained in place I would never be able to forgive her from my heart. You can't curse someone and love them at the same time.

God is telling us in this commandment that if we pass judgment on our parents and speak dishonoring words about them, things will not go well for us. Even though we may be, in our own eyes, justifiably angry towards them, our judgmental and dishonoring words and actions only serve to give the enemy legal ground that he can use against us. Our judgments cut us off from the providence and favour of God.

What does judging our parents look like? It is when we say, "What they did was wrong—they owe me." Every child knows that when they purposely do something wrong their parents will punish them, and that punishment is justifiable. But when we feel our parents' actions were unfair and unjustified, that's when we make the judgment call. We think, no that is wrong and unfair, I hate you for that! But God commands us that we should not dishonor our parents by judging or despising them in this way.

It is important here to understand that God is not telling us we should endure any kind of abuse from our parents and simply put up with it. How, for instance, could someone endure their parent consistently beating or abusing them and still honor them? What this verse means is not that God wants us to tolerate ungodly behavior from our parents and not challenge it, but that He asks us to honor their *position* as our parents, despite their actions. God wants us to honor our mother and father who, if nothing else, were responsible for bringing us into this world. We honor their position of authority in God, which is not the same as endorsing their actions—they are responsible to God for their own actions.

In Matthew 7:1 Jesus confirms,

"Do not judge, or you too will be judged. For in the same way you judge others, you will be judged, and with the measure you use, it will be measured to you."

MATTHEW 7:1-2

And similarly, Romans 2:1 says,

"You, therefore, have no excuse, you who pass judgment on someone else, for at whatever point you judge the other, you are condemning yourself, because you who pass judgment do the same things."

How often do we catch ourselves doing something that we dislike and complain about in others? When we condemn them we are condemning ourselves! Galatians 6:7 corroborates these truths, saying, *"Do not be deceived: God cannot be mocked. A man reaps what he sows. "*

Obviously these are not among our top ten favorite Bible verses! But they contain powerful truths we must heed. In the natural realm if we plant one seed in the ground we expect to reap a multiplied harvest. If we plant a single seed of corn and only reap back one or two corn seeds, that is a terrible harvest! We expect lots of kernels to grow from that one seed. That is God's law of increase. Similarly, in the spiritual realm, if we sow seeds of love, joy, generosity, kindness, goodness, forgiveness and mercy we will reap an abundance of those things back. But if we sow seeds of anger, judgment, bitterness, gossip and violence, we will also reap those things back, but in increasing intensity, like a bumper crop of weeds.

THE GARDENER OF THE HEART

Although I had been terribly hurt by my mother's actions over the years, I knew that I needed to go and ask her forgiveness for the many times I had dishonored and judged her. The Holy Spirit was revealing to me that this would be an important key to unlocking and releasing my hurt and receiving God's healing and blessing. So I went to see her and attempted to raise the subject. I chose my words carefully and said, "Mom, I've realized that I have dishonored you and judged you in anger and bitterness all these years. Now I want to work through some of these issues with you and ask you to forgive me."

But, as soon as I said those words to her my mother said, "Stop! Don't ever mention this to me again. I'm too old, too much has happened, and I don't want to deal with it. Never mention it again!"

I was horrified by her reaction. I had thought, yes, this is the way in which I am going to be set free from all my bitterness, and now my hopes seemed to be dashed. How was I going to work through this and get my heart restored, I wondered? Then God said to me, "If you are really serious about this, then give me permission to dig in the garden of your heart. Give me permission to show you the roots, to bring up the situations you need to deal with one at a time."

Of course, I gave the Holy Spirit permission and that began what was to be a three and a half year process towards freedom, with me allowing Him to raise and deal with issue after issue, in His way and in His time. Often, it could be five or ten times a day, the Lord would bring something up from my past and speak to me about it, and I knew immediately where He was going with it and what He was after. Some were pretty tiny, insignificant things, that I hadn't thought about for years and others were major issues. Each time He would ask me, "Did you honor or dishonor in that situation?"

Of course, I had pretty much always dishonored my mother in those situations, so I would first acknowledge my own sin of judgment against her, then I would speak out forgiveness for her for that specific incident at that specific time. I gave her a gift of forgiveness for each situation and said, "Mom, you owe me nothing for that. I lay it all down at the foot of the cross." While I worked through this process, my relationship with my mom continued to be testing. I would call her on the phone like any daughter would and say, "Hi Mom, how are you today?" and my mother would typically control and manipulate. One time she answered, "Who's this?"

"It's Carol, Mom," I said.

"Carol who?"

Well, my mom only has one daughter—me! In fact, she only has one child! She was upset because I hadn't called her for two or three days. It seemed to me that our relationship would continue to be dysfunctional and that I would still be controlled by her words, still afraid of how she would react.

TWO-WAY FORGIVENESS

With the Holy Spirit's help, I began to understand more and more that forgiveness—any and every kind of forgiveness—is a two-way deal. When someone hurts or attacks us in life, we tend only to be concerned with the sin that has been committed against us, but behind that is our own sinful reaction to that sin. It is that sin that we commit as a result of the sin that was carried out against us that, if not dealt with, will pull us out of God's grace and bring us back down to the justice level (as discussed in the first section of this book).

If we try to operate on the justice level instead of living in the freedom of God's grace then the enemy has every right to inflict the full power of the law of sowing and reaping against us. What does this mean in reality? It sets in motion a terrible cycle, such as in the following scenario: One person sins against us by being judgmental and critical of us behind our back. We get to hear about it and we are, in our eyes, justifiably offended and hurt by their remarks. We react badly and speak out judgments and criticism about them—"Who are they to criticize me? What about all their faults? etc." Later we feel bad and decide that, because it's the "right" thing to do, we will forgive them. We say a few words about it to the Lord and we think that is that, but we have neglected to deal with the issue of our own sin, our judgments.

What happens now is that having sown in judgment and criticism, we begin to reap some of that back. Another person judges and criticizes us and we can't quite believe it is happening again. "What? Now this person is attacking me? Why is this happening?" Usually we are blind to the fact that our own sinful reaction is setting us up to become trapped in this ongoing vicious circle.

As the Lord began to help me to understand these things I thought more about my mother and the way in which she reacted to me, her child. I could only come to the conclusion that her behavior was not that of a person who was just utterly dysfunctional, but must be the result of events in her own life, and of how she herself had chosen to react to them. So I began to ask questions. I wanted to get to the bottom of what had shaped Mom into the person I knew. Of course, my mother was completely unwilling to discuss it, so I couldn't go to her, so I began to ask questions of my aunts. I asked them, what was *your* mother like? What was your father like? And little by little I began to build up a picture. This is what I discovered...

My mother grew up in really hard times in the midst of the

Depression. The family lived on a farm and she was the youngest of seven children. She had two brothers and four sisters. After child number six was born her mom didn't really want to be pregnant again—she felt she had to be out in the fields working hard alongside her husband. But, when she became pregnant a seventh time and resigned herself to the fact, then she was determined that it had to be a boy. She didn't want another little girl, she wanted a boy who would be able to work on the farm. So on two counts, my mom was unwanted.

But to make matters worse, after she was born her sisters had to bring her up. Her mother left her for most of the time and went to work in the fields. Mom's older sisters were already mostly responsible for raising a couple of the younger children, so they were not happy about this new arrival, and as a result they were frequently cruel to her. Once when she was three years old they locked her in a closet for several hours just because she had been crying. My mom had no one to turn to, so her only means of survival was to harden her heart. She sought to protect herself emotionally by developing and using the tools of anger, domination, manipulation and control.

Learning about her circumstances and beginning to appreciate what had made her into the person I knew, opened the door to a godly compassion I didn't think I was capable of. I continued to work through all the issues I had, one after another, with the Holy Spirit's help and three years went by. My mom and I lived in the same city and as her only child I tried hard to love and honor her. One day, when I went to visit her, just as I was leaving, I gave her a big hug and said, "Mom, I love you." In my heart my words were not a lie, because I was trying to express love for her the best way I could. But then, one day, after this three year journey, all of a sudden out of nowhere, an incredible love for my mother flooded into my heart. I then knew for certain that at that moment Jesus had completely healed me and set me free from the vicious cycle of judgment I had been imprisoned within.

In Matthew 18:18 Jesus teaches that whatever we bind on earth will be bound in heaven, and whatever we loose on earth will be loosed in heaven. Because I was able to loose my mom of all the terrible judgments I had spoken against her, another miracle occurred: it allowed the Holy Spirit to begin to work in her life as well as my own.

There was an immediate and dramatic change in my mother's behavior. She was perhaps 90% of the way towards being completely set free—to my utter amazement! Our relationship improved right away and on the days when she was difficult, I was able to quickly forgive her. Even if there was a more serious blip in our relationship, the longest time I was ever upset about it was one day. Always at the forefront of my mind was this: "Get over it, Carol. Forgive her. You do not want to go back into justice. Stay in grace!" So I gave my mom the gift of forgiveness and said to her in my heart, "Mom, I forgive you. You owe me nothing." Jesus said in John 20:23, *"If you forgive the sins of any, they are forgiven them. And if you retain the sins of any, they are retained."* (NASB) It was amazing to see the truth of that Scripture in action and eventually I had the joy of seeing my mom become a believer in Jesus.

One day I received a phone call from my father. He had been diagnosed with bladder cancer and needed to be admitted to hospital for treatment. Because he had to go to another city to receive his treatment he would be gone for a while and he wanted me to look after Mom in his absence. My mom needed regular care because of a stroke she'd had years earlier.

That incident in itself had been a strange occurrence. She had suffered a major stroke at the age of 55, despite the fact that she didn't have high blood pressure or any of the other symptoms normally associated with stroke victims. She was, however, furious with her neighbor. They had fallen out over some matter; no one knew quite what it was and she was so angry that she had forbidden my dad to speak to him. One day, whilst my dad was in the garden trimming the hedge, the neighbor approached him and my mom came out of the house and had a real row with him. After that she suffered a major stroke and, as a result, the right side of her body became paralyzed.

I now found myself caring for Mom in her home while Dad was away. One day, my best friend Judy came by the house to bring me something and, for some unknown reason, my mom was really horrible to her. I was stunned. My usual modus operandi with Mom was to avoid direct confrontation because of her tendency to explode with anger, but this day I felt the Holy Spirit gently urging me to talk to her about what had happened. It took Him three days of gentle but insistent prompting before I was ready to address the issue, but eventually I spoke to Mom about it. "Mom, you're a Christian now. The way you treated Judy the other day was horrible. What was all that about?"

Mom defended her actions, "Well, she walked right by me at church on Sunday morning and didn't even speak!" That was what had made her angry.

"But Mom," I said, "that doesn't deserve that kind of treatment."

"Well," she huffed in response, "she is a very domineering and manipulative person anyway!"

As soon as she said those words I said, "Right Mom! So, tell me what your mother was like; what your sisters were like; what every person in your life who ever hurt you was like." The moment I spoke out those words the floodgates burst. Guess what! They were dominating, controlling and angry towards her. For the next two and a half hours my mom, who at this point was 89 years old, wept and wept. She forgave her mother, forgave her sisters, and forgave all the people in her life who had hurt her—including my friend Judy.

Afterwards I told her, "Mom, if you are really serious about what we've just prayed about, I want you to phone Judy and tell her you're sorry." Now, my mom had never said sorry to anyone, ever, her whole life, so what I was asking her to do presented a major challenge. But, about three weeks later I received a phone call from Judy asking me to meet her for lunch. By then I had almost forgotten about the incident. I checked with my mom that she would be OK if I left her for a short while and then went to meet Judy, who told me, "You'll never guess what! Your mom called me and apologized!" I said, "Alright, God!" It was a huge miracle and I was very excited.

This little episode may seem insignificant to some, but it paved the way for a greater miracle to take place. I returned to the house after lunch and my mom was being really miserable and grumpy. "What's the matter, Mom?" I asked. "I thought you were OK with me going out to lunch with Judy? Anyway, Mom, Judy said you phoned and apologized to her—that's great, Mom!"

"Well," Mom retorted, "I'm mad at Judy again."

"Why?" I wanted to know.

"Because she walked right by me again on Sunday morning."

"Mom," I said, "do you know that the enemy wants to bring you back down to the justice level? Do you remember a long time ago I came to you and wanted to talk through the issues where I had judged you?"

"No," she said.

"You do too!" I said and immediately she broke down in tears.

"Carol," she said. "I am so sorry. The very thing that was done to me I've done to you."

Then my mom and I got to hug and *truly* forgive one another. It was an incredible moment. Our relationship has been completely transformed. Now she tells me on the phone, "I love you" even before I can say it to her. She tells me, "I'm proud of you." It is a miracle because God gave me my mom back—a loving mom that I had never had. Forgiveness works!

—

The problems I experienced with my mother because of the judgments I had spoken over her were not the only problems I had. Whenever we sow seeds of judgment and criticism, we reap them back manifold. As well as having a dysfunctional relationship with my mom, therefore, I also reaped through domineering, controlling and manipulative women in the church. At times I felt as though there was a sign above my head in the spiritual realm saying, "Controlling, manipulative women wanted—come and practice on me!"

I do have a measure of spiritual discernment, but in this area of my life it was like I had blinders on. I could never see it coming. I had friendships with several different ladies in the church and I would embrace them and love them, but it was never long before they were using me to do something or get something they wanted and I always ended up being controlled, manipulated and hurt. The result of this was that I began to create security measures to guard my emotions until finally I had built a wall around my heart that would not let anyone else in.

This also affected my relationship with John. I knew that he really loved me and would do anything for me; he would stand up for me in any situation. But in this one area, it was like John had blinders on too. He just could not see the problem. It was driving me crazy. Week after week at church someone would approach me and begin to burden me with their latest gossip, taking advantage of our friendship to tell me who had done what and who had said what, and did I know this was happening in the church? I would go to John and tell him about it and it was as though he was deaf! I would say, "John, this is really serious" and he would respond, "Oh, you're probably exaggerating" or "Oh, you must have heard that wrong." One time he even said, "Oh, maybe you're jealous," which made me furious—but I forgave him!

Some may argue that perhaps our church had more than its fair share of manipulative people, but not only did this happen in that first church we were pastoring, it happened in the other church we planted in Toronto around that time. We were looking after both churches simultaneously and the situation was being replicated. I began to pray about it more seriously, because I was so concerned. "God, what is going on? I don't understand this situation. I don't understand John's reaction to me—it just goes against who John is and what he is like." Eventually God spoke to me and said, simply, "Carol, you've judged your father." I was a little taken aback by this statement. I then spent several minutes telling God how great I thought my dad was, how wonderful he was and how I adored him. But then I stopped and God was totally silent. Eventually I asked Him, "Lord, is there something I have judged my father for? What is it, Father?" and He said to me, "You've judged your father because he did not protect you from your mother." After reflecting on this for a while I really felt God was telling me that this judgment had bound someone who really loved me—John—from protecting me against the worst aspects of "mother" church. If you find that statement difficult to swallow, I have to say that my first reaction was, "Oh, Lord, that's really far fetched. That's really stretching it isn't it?" I was very unsure, so I decided to meet up with a girlfriend of mine who I really trust and talk it over with her. "This is what I think God may be saying to me," I told her. "It sounds way out there to me, but I want to be accountable. Will you work through it with me?" We decided together that the best thing to do was for me to pray and offer forgiveness. So I forgave my dad and released him from any judgment, and I forgave John and released him from judgment. Then I kind of forgot about the issue for a while.

A little time went by and then a situation flared up in the church which, again, I found myself caught up in. I went to talk to John about it and said, "Honey, this has happened and I think it's really serious. We ought to deal with it." I was amazed by John's reaction. Immediately he said, "What! You're kidding me? I'll bring that person in right now and we'll deal with that situation right now!" His whole attitude towards the issue had changed dramatically and it was as though the blinders had been removed and he could clearly see the problem.

This is how powerful judgments made in hurt and bitterness can be. Judgments of dishonor give Satan a legal right to bring all kinds of things against you. Do you have a sign over your head in the spiritual realm? Are you always being passed over? Are you always being rejected? Do people verbally abuse you? Have you been physically abused? Do you feel that people never notice what you do and never affirm you? Maybe you are like I was, always being controlled and manipulated then hurt and spit out?

God cares about you so much that He doesn't want such a situation to continue in your life. He wants you to be healed and completely set free from bondage. God took the trouble to help my mother become free from the bondage that had crippled her emotionally. He began and He completed the process, even though she was 89 years old. It is never too late. God does not want the debilitating power of judgment to limit us. He wants us to soak in His river of grace and enjoy all the blessings He has for us. We have tapped into but a fraction of all that God has for us, but that's not because of His heart, it's because of ours—because of the blockages in our lives that prevent the River of Grace from flowing there.

THE POWER OF FORGIVENESS TO BRING RELEASE

Forgiveness is often the starting point of freedom. Today you may find yourself in the worst situation imaginable and you cannot see how forgiveness can take place, but God is willing and able to help you. Maybe your son was murdered or your daughter raped, or some other horrific situation occurred in your life and you cannot bring yourself to forgive the perpetrators? Maybe your issue is a lot less serious than any of these, but nevertheless you still feel bound up by it and are suffering emotionally? I hope you can relate to the hurts that I had and are encouraged that, however grave the situation, our God is able to turn your situation around. The Holy Spirit can minister into your life and bring you up into the place of grace and freedom.

I have seen God turn around many failing marriages with the power of forgiveness. Once John and I were approached by a pastor and his wife in Mexico. The lady said to us, "I don't even know why I'm telling you this, but I'm leaving my husband."

"Why?" I asked, "You're pastors! Tell me the story, what has happened?"

She told us that her husband beat her violently almost every week. She said that each time he did it, soon after he was full of remorse and promised never to do it again, but it just kept on happening. "I can't stand any more of it," she said, "so I'm leaving."

I looked at this poor couple and then addressed the man. "Sir," I said, "tell me what your dad was like." Immediately he hung his head, full of shame and hurt. "He used to beat my mother," he confessed.

"Sir, that's your problem," I said. "You have judged your father and now you are doing the very same thing."

We prayed with them and I asked the husband to pray a prayer with me and to give his dad a gift of forgiveness. Although his father was no longer alive, he still needed to forgive him. Something broke through spiritually. We finished praying with these dear people and then went our separate ways.

Several years went by and we bumped into this couple again. They came running up to us and said, "Do you remember us?" The lady told me, "I was going to leave my husband because he used to beat me all the time. He hasn't beaten me since that day you prayed with us." Forgiveness was released and the bondage was broken; mercy had triumphed over judgment (James 2:13).

A few years ago John was teaching this message at a church in Chicago. A lady came to him at the end of the service responding to the call for ministry and allowed God to deal with many issues in her life. She then went to visit her 93 year old mother who was in a nursing home. She had a powerful time of prayer and healing with her mom, who then so "caught" the message of forgiveness that she decided she must be reconciled to her sister-in-law. She telephoned and asked forgiveness of a lady she had not spoken to for 75 years over a family disagreement!

So far we have discussed forgiveness and breaking judgments only in personal terms between individuals, but the principles of forgiveness can also apply to families, churches, communities, nations and even entire ethnic groups. Some of the terrible situations that have occurred around the world bear testament to the fact that this is true. South Africa has a long history of ethnic conflict as does the Balkan region of Europe. But ethnic hatred is not a new problem. In the 13th Century B.C. the ancient Assyrians adopted a policy of displacing any restless minority groups to other lands. It goes back to the beginnings of civilization.

When people judge that one ethnic group has perpetrated injustice on another ethnic group, that just empowers the devil to make similar violence happen again and again. But there is power in the act of forgiveness for an ethnic group and in the act of repentance on behalf of an ethnic group, just as there is for individuals. Once at a conference in Germany we felt prompted by the Holy Spirit to lead the people in a prayer of forgiveness for ancestors who had been involved in the events of World War II and particularly the Holocaust. People who were suffering the effects of judgments made against them for being German were wonderfully liberated by God as the floodgates opened. Freedom came in as they forgave their ancestors, their nation and themselves for the shame over their nation.

PRAYERS FOR
RELEASING FORGIVENESS

Reflect on the following thought for a few minutes:

How many readers would like to be *exactly* like your father or *exactly* like your mother? Highlight the areas in which you would definitely *not* want to be like them and write them down. Now think about what you have written. It is possible that, in the areas where you don't want to copy the pattern laid down by your father/mother, you have judged them and there may be a root of bitterness and dishonor attached to those areas.

It may be, for instance, that you struggle with worry, even though you have told yourself that you are determined not to be a worrier, because your mother always worried about everything. It is very likely that you judged and dishonored her, dismissing her tendency to worry as her being neurotic. But now you are reaping the consequences of that judgment yourself and being swamped by your own irrational worries. The solution to this is to repent of having judged her and forgive and release her for how her actions have affected you, both now and in the past.

This is one simple example, but during the course of reading this book no doubt the Holy Spirit has highlighted different things in your heart. You may need to forgive someone as He has prompted you to do so. It is quite likely that you also need to forgive yourself for things you've done in the past that you are ashamed of. Sometimes we do terrible things, but having repented of them we need to learn to forgive ourselves just as God forgives us. It doesn't matter how bad the thing is in your eyes—whether you have committed adultery or had an abortion—if you have truly repented then God has truly forgiven you. I have heard people say, "Oh, I am sure God has forgiven me, but I cannot forgive myself." Don't be more righteous than the Lord! If He is satisfied, who are you to hold onto it? Sometimes we need to make restitution for past sins if it is possible to do so, because this is a biblical principle. Sometimes it is simply not possible. But in either case, if God has forgiven us then we need to forgive ourselves and step into the grace of God.

Sometimes people even blame God when bad things happen to them. There is a sense in which some people need to "forgive God" (even though God did nothing wrong because He is never responsible for sin). Often, when God doesn't answer someone's prayers in the way they hoped He would, they can become resentful or angry with Him. This is something that we definitely need to let go of as well.

Below you will find prayers to guide and assist you in praying through these areas. The issues we face are so diverse that they can never cover every situation adequately, but they will serve as templates to help you begin to dialogue with God about your specific problems. Above all remember this: give the Holy Spirit permission to come and dig in the garden of your heart. Rather than becoming self-critical and analyzing things which may not be relevant, allow Him to bring up the issues that are important. His heart is to bring you to a place of complete freedom, so He will address the areas of your life in which you are bound up. He is faithful and He wants you to be free to bathe in the river of God's grace and mercy.

PRAYER TO FORGIVE PARENTS

For your father:

Heavenly Father, I come to you in surrender today and I truly want to deal with the issue you have been gently prompting me about. Lord, I want to give my father a gift of my forgiveness today—for all the things that you did or didn't do which caused me pain and also caused me to judge you in ungodliness.

[Imagine your father and say]

Dad, I forgive you for... [tell the Lord the specific things you forgive him for—the abuse, the abandonment, the criticisms]. I give you a gift of my forgiveness. You owe me nothing. I tear up the i.o.u. that I had written in my heart and I give it all to you, Heavenly Father. I bring it to the cross and, Lord, I ask you to forgive me for my sin of dishonoring, judging and hating my dad in my heart. Lord, I repent and I ask you to forgive me. Lord, I put the cross of Jesus between me and the law of sowing and reaping. I don't want to reap negativity any more.

For your mother:

Lord, I choose today to forgive my mother. Mom, I forgive you for... [tell the Lord what it's for]. I let it go today. I tear up the i.o.u. Lord, I want to be free. I let it all go to the cross. Lord, I ask you to forgive me for judging my mother; for dishonoring her. Lord, that is sin and I repent of it.

Lord, I take my freedom today. I step up into the grace of God. Lord, I want to give others a gift of my forgiveness. I forgive my brothers and my sisters. I forgive my uncles, aunts, grandparents and other family members. I forgive my school teachers. I forgive my peers growing up in school. I forgive my bosses. I forgive my ex-girlfriend or boyfriend. I forgive my husband or wife. I forgive my pastors and church friends.

Lord, I forgive everyone who has hurt me and I tear up the i.o.u's. All of those injustices—I tear them up and lay them at the foot of the cross and ask you Lord to forgive me for my sins of judging. Lord, I want to be free and I receive my freedom now.

PRAYER TO FORGIVE OURSELVES

Lord, I choose today to give myself a gift of my own forgiveness. [Say your own name]. I let it go. I forgive you for [tell the Lord what it is]. I let it go and I forgive myself. I will not beat myself up about it any more and I release it to you, Lord Jesus. I can't be the Savior for myself. Lord, you are my Savior.

Take a deep breath and let out all the striving, all the condemnation you have put yourself through. Hand over all that controlling fear to Jesus. Just step into your Heavenly Daddy's arms right now, into His rest, experience His peace and realize that it's all paid for—your freedom is all paid for by Jesus. There is nothing more for you to do except believe that it has all been done (John 3:16). Forgive and you shall be forgiven. Thank you, Lord.

A PRAYER TO SAY SORRY TO GOD
FOR BLAMING HIM

Once a very angry man said to me, "Where was the God of
love when my friend's eight year old girl was run down and
killed by a drunk driver?" I said, "Sir, did God force that guy
to drink until he was drunk and then get into his car and
drive? That was not God, that was sin." Sin has consequences,
that's why God hates sin. And when we are the victim we are
so in touch with how wrong it is aren't we? When we are the
perpetrator we tend to minimize sin and don't realize what it
has done to hurt God and hurt others. But so often we blame
God when people sin. You may say, "But if He is all-powerful,
then why did He allow it?" For the same reason he "allowed"
you to sin. God has given us a free will, yet we are responsible
for our own actions. Don't blame God for the sinful choices
of others. Let's pray...

> Lord Jesus, I have wrongly blamed you for things that have
> happened to me and the circumstances of my life [tell God
> about specific instances where this has been an issue for you].

> Father, forgive me, Lord, for when I blamed You for these
> things. I no longer blame You and I accept your mercy and
> grace.

A PRAYER TO BREAK THE BONDAGE
OF JUDGMENTS OVER THOSE WHO HURT US

John 10:10 says the enemy is a thief who comes to steal, kill
and destroy. But Jesus has broken the power of the enemy and
overwritten that curse of death with His own life. In the same
verse He affirms, "*I have come that you might have life and have*

it more abundantly." This means that we need to take a giant step into the grace of God and stop living a life limited by the bondage of judgments.

After having prayed a prayer of forgiveness for those who have hurt you, and having repented of judging them, pray the following prayer of release. Rise up in your authority as a believer and free yourself from these situations!

Father, in the name of Jesus, I cut myself free from every soulish, ungodly tie to every person who has sinned against me, who has ever hurt me, who has abused me either emotionally or physically in any way. I sever those unholy ties now in the name of Jesus and I free myself from their control.

Father, I free myself from every bit of demonic oppression that has come to me down the generational stream of my family. Thank you that the blood of Jesus Christ, God's Son, frees me from control, witchcraft, fear, violence, shame, abuse and pain. There is now no condemnation for me as I am in Christ Jesus. Not because I deserve that, Lord, but because it is a free gift to me from You.

It has all been paid for by your Son, Jesus. Thank You, Lord!

I step forward now and take hold of the freedom you have won for me, Lord Jesus. I receive the grace of God. Thank you that this is part of my inheritance in Christ. I affirm my identity in your Son Jesus and I thank you that I am a new creation in Him. The law of the Spirit of life in Christ Jesus has set me free from the law of sin and death. I take my freedom! (Romans 8:2)

ABOUT THE AUTHORS

John and Carol Arnott are the Founding Pastors of Catch The Fire Toronto (formerly known as Toronto Airport Christian Fellowship) and are Presidents of Catch The Fire World. They are also overseers of the Partners in Harvest network of churches around the world. As international speakers, John and Carol have become known for their ministry of revival in the context of the Father's saving and restoring love. As the Holy Spirit moves with signs and wonders, they have seen millions of lives touched and changed through God's power and Christ's love.

John attended Ontario Bible College (now Tyndale College) in the late 1960s and then pursued a successful career in business. In 1980, while on a ministry trip to Indonesia, John and Carol responded to God's call on their lives for full-time ministry. Upon returning home, they started Jubilee Christian Fellowship in Stratford, Ontario in 1981. The Lord then called them to Toronto in 1987, where Toronto Airport Christian

Fellowship was started. In January 1994, through a sovereign outpouring of the Holy Spirit, revival exploded into protracted nightly meetings which continued for 12 years, as the church came to the world's attention as a place where God was meeting with His people.

John is known for his teachings on the Father's love, grace and forgiveness and the Holy Spirit's power. He continues to impart wise counsel and provides a strong framework for those who want to see the power of God manifest in their church. Carol is especially known for her teachings on intimacy and soaking.

John and Carol live north of Toronto. They travel extensively while continuing to oversee Catch The Fire and Partners in Harvest networks of churches.

Catch The Fire Toronto is now a city-wide church in Toronto with multiple campuses and thousands of vibrant members from many diverse and ethnic backgrounds.

Catch The Fire World is an international ministry involved in church planting, conferences and events, training schools, missions work and media outreach. Partners in Harvest and Friends in Harvest is a church network of over 500 churches internationally in over 50 nations.

YOU WERE MADE FOR MORE

A God who
loves you

wants you to
experience him

be transformed

and given
power

At Catch The Fire, we are passionate about seeing people be transformed by a living God. We have many books that can help you on your journey, but we are also involved in much more.

Why not join us at a conference or seminar this year? Or come on a short-term mission with us? Or have your heart radically changed at a 5-month school. Or just visit one of our churches in many cities around the world.

CONTINUE YOUR JOURNEY AT

catchthefirebooks.com/whatsnext

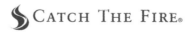

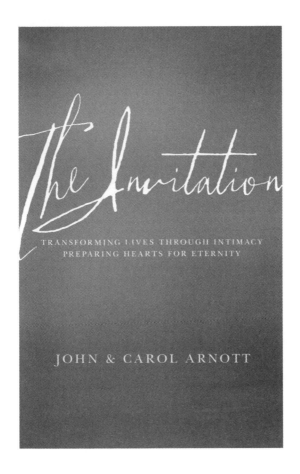

THE INVITATION
JOHN & CAROL ARNOTT

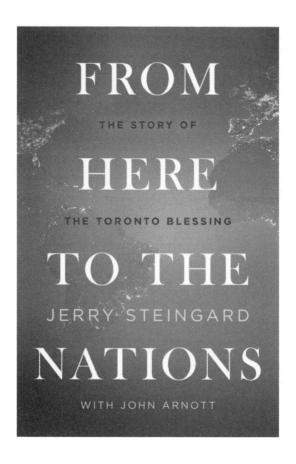

THE POWER OF THANKSGIVING
FRED & SHARON WRIGHT